T0063555

Feminine, Free, and Faithful

Feminine, Free, and Faithful

Single but Free

Rosa Mary Lucio

WESTBOW
PRESS®
A DIVISION OF THOMAS NELSON
& ZONDERVAN

Scripture quotations are taken from the Complete Jewish Bible, copyright ©
1998 by David H. Stern. Published by Jewish New Testament Publications,
Inc. www.messianicjewish.net/jntp. Distributed by Messianic Jewish Resources.
www.messianicjewish.net. All rights reserved. Used by permission.

Scripture taken from the King James Version of the Bible.

WestBow Press books may be ordered through booksellers or by contacting:

WestBow Press
A Division of Thomas Nelson & Zondervan
1663 Liberty Drive
Bloomington, IN 47403
www.westbowpress.com
1 (866) 928-1240

ISBN: 978-1-4908-9787-5 (sc)
ISBN: 978-1-4908-9788-2 (e)

Print information available on the last page.

WestBow Press rev. date: 05/03/2016

Dedication

To the lady that helped mold and shape my life. This wonderful lady also stressed education, morality with dignity and self respect. To my mama Alise Mae Robinson

Table of Contents

Introduction

*T*here is a vital need in the Body of Christ and also in the secular world to differentiate between a godly woman and a woman of worldly means. This book is written to advise both entities that God still has single women that live and have Holy standards. These single women of El Elyon the highest God have not bowed down to the Baal's or little gods of this world. Their reverential fear is to God in whom they have decided to trust. These single women have decided to follow God, and His Holy Commandments; therefore, they have made a commitment to constantly abide in and by His Holy Word. So to the Christian women who know that there will be changes in their lives, I applaud you for your Christian stalwartness and point of view in these evil days. These single women can endure, shoulder, stand, swallow, and tolerate, because of their knowledge of God's grace in their lives. Therefore, their state of affairs has not hindered them, because their assurance is that they are prize-winning overcomers. Single Christian women you shall receive a crown of life.

> "Blessed is the man that endureth temptation; for when he is tried, he shall receive the crown of life, which the Lord hath promised them that love him". (James 1:12).

Why?

*M*any Christian women know that there will be some fluctuation in their lives. But as Christian women we have the word of God to help us conquer and defeat the most extreme circumstances. This book is not for most women, but for the Christian woman, that is waiting for her Boaz. This woman hopes to embrace the marriage vows soon with the right person, and this woman has decided to wait on God. This woman of God that is free continues beyond all odds to be consistent in her faithfulness to God. She has not seen the God of her life with her natural eyes, but has come to know him in a very special way with her spiritual insight. She loves him because this God of many other Christian women ascertain no fault in her past, present or future endeavors. God has assured her that she has no guilt or shame because of bad mistakes and misfortunes in her life. She has accepted Christ in her life and all sins are forgiven. For the reason that God is God, her redeemer; this woman has decided to be feminine, free, and faithful to Him. Her number one priority is to live a godly life. Therefore, she may experience some consequences of being feminine, free, and faithful.

CHAPTER I

The Woman
What Is A Woman?

The World Book Dictionary Definition:

*W*oman (n) as a female human being, a woman is a grown up girl. Women as a group; the average woman or womankind, women's nature womanliness; (Adj) of a woman or women; feminine; (Syn) (N) women, lady,—means member of the feminine sex, a woman of high ideas. Lady applies particular to a woman of refinement or high social position. A woman is born a 'baby girl'.

The Word of God says. "And Adam, said, This is now bone of my bones, and flesh of my flesh: she shall be called Woman, because she was taken out of Man." Genesis 2:23

The spoken and living Word of God specifically tells us that God himself recognize that his creation here on earth by the name of Adam needed someone in his life. In Genesis 2:21-22, we become spiritually and intellectually aware that God put Adam into a deep sleep, and then he took a rib from the man's rib cage. And God made the man a woman, and brought her to the man. As the result of this miraculous surgery by the hand of God we know that God did not make woman for another woman, nor did he make man for another man. God is not confused in his creative ability of mankind. A woman is not a man dressed up in women clothes, neither is a woman a transsexual, neither is a woman an original man which by the hands of evil mankind changes his masculine sex to create and form what this person normally was not born to be or with. The former definition let us know that a woman is a grown up girl, not a grown up boy who wants to be a girl. Let's keep things in their right perspective. A woman is a feminine creature that has high ideas. This woman is not going to stop here but she is pressing towards being a refined lady of high social moral values. The woman that Jehovah Elohim created was exactly what the man Adam needed. Her Hebrew name Ishshah means-a woman, a mortal, taking from another. Therefore, the woman that God created for Adam was not of the female gender of a domestic animal such as: a cat, a dog, a cow, a chicken, a horse or a donkey. The Word of God declares;

> "Thou shalt not lie with mankind as with womankind: it is abomination. Neither shalt thou lie with any beast to defile thyself therewith: neither shall any woman stand before a beast to lie down thereto: it is confusion." (Leviticus 18:22-23) From the Abingdon's Strong's Exhaustive Concordance of the Bible: The word confusion means it is unnatural, perverse, disorder, a lack of clarity.

Henceforth, with the definition above the beloved women of God should not allow the persuasions and evil desires of the world pull them from under the protecting arms of Almighty God, neither should they be compelled to let go of the perfect will of God.

CHAPTER II

The Feminine Woman

T he woman has played many roles in various societies throughout history. She has been a wife, a mother, a farmer, a laborer, a business executive, a teacher, and also a volunteer worker. Most women have accomplished and combined two or more of these daily roles into their lives. Throughout the centuries, almost every society has developed specific ideas of what activities are suitable for women. Some societies have given women honor and fame. While others have considered and treated women with defamatory behaviors, sometimes lower animals have received better treatments.

Most societies have associated their ideas about women with farfetched beliefs regarding women outer appearances. Women have been looked upon as objects of honor or dishonor depending on how the observer sees them. The size of their bodies maybe slim or wide fat or thin. These beliefs of how women outward appearance should be have had no scientific or spiritual foundation regarding femininity. Erroneous beliefs about the lustful appetizing desires of a woman's flesh has been accepted for so many years that women sometimes fail to question what is their feminine role in society. Motherhood has played a major part in determining a woman's feminine place in society. A woman has also been evaluated because of her size and strength, her emotions and temperaments. How strange our society is today, how society hardly looks at a woman's inner godly femininity. Our society looks at a woman for what she has to offer outwardly whether good or bad. The feminine woman of God is not what man wants or has created for his own selfish desires.

This feminine woman has been created to be dainty in every area of her life. To be feminine is to forget about what man and society wants you to be, but what God wants you to be. A feminine woman should show attributes of being delicate, stylish and graceful and spiritual. This woman should be pleasing to the eye. She should be well groomed, well dressed, and well designed. Her gracefulness is her number one attribute of who she really is. The feminine woman should have an air of being well poised and well balanced. She should not be double minded, because this will show that she is unstable in all her ways. Her charm should be friendly delightful, warm and sociable.

Her very presence should represent God. Therefore, being beautiful is the traditional norm for her. She is fantastic, her very aroma and fragrance is exquisite. She is appealing, enchanting, and pleasant to be near. She is so lovely, that her beauty is Divine and heavenly. A feminine woman is not vulgar, coarse, awkward or dull. She is not disagreeable, unfriendly, dreadful, offensive in her manner, nor earthly. She does not seek the devilish wisdom of this world. She daily seeks the wisdom of God. Her favorite daily Bible scripture is from James 3:17 which says, "But the wisdom that is from above is first, pure, then peaceable, gentle, and easy to entreated, full of mercy and good fruits, without partiality, and without hypocrisy."

The feminine woman is proper, discreet, and polite. Even though she may not be likable by some, she is relish by many. The feminine woman in today's society must believe that God wants them to be feminine in every aspect of their lives. Although, there are many roles that society has tried to place upon this woman. This woman of Divine excellence and Divine beauty knows her place in God. This woman of God knows the reasons for her existence.

The feminine Christian woman knows her place in God. She is not intimated by the standards of the world. She knows that the Word of God says, "That he will beautify the meek with salvation."

Being feminine is an highlighted trait that God has put in all women. There is no need to want to look and act like a man—femme. We single Christian women should want to, and truly desire to be beautiful and feminine for our God and Creator-Jehovah Elohim. God in His Divine creativity made woman for man, not man for woman. He did not even make or fashion a woman for another woman. Being out of the will of God is not what God has planned for our lives. If you are a woman and you are involved with another human being that God did not create you for, please go to the altar of repentance and prostrate yourself before the God of all Grace to ask for forgiveness and much needed deliverance. There are some things that are an abomination before the very presence of God. God is not confused or perplex, the word of God says, "And the rib, which the Lord God had taken from man, made he a woman, and brought her unto the man." (Genesis 2:22)

Therefore, if the single Christian woman has anticipation of embracing the wedding vows she should present herself attractive at all times to the opposite sex. BE FEMININE! This feminine woman does not have the desire to be faithful to others that do not have the righteousness of God in their view. Because this feminine woman loves God with all her heart she says 'no' to the thoughts that will bring the wrath of God in her life, because of the lust of the eyes, the lust of the flesh, and the pride of life. She recognizes that she, Ishshah, is waiting on her Ish (husband).

The feminine Christian woman will remain pure before her God. Her confidence is in God's Word, which declares:

"For the which cause I also suffer those things: nevertheless I am not ashamed: for I know whom I have believed, and am persuaded that he is able to keep that which I have committed unto Him against that day." II Timothy 2:12

This feminine woman is the very persona of Jesus Christ. She avoids anything and any one that is foul-mouthed and bad mannered. Her perception of others is love; therefore, she has little or no tolerance for someone being thoughtless, and ruthless with negligence to others.

CHAPTER III

The Worldly Woman

*T*he woman of the world desires are to be enriched by her selfish ambitions. She doesn't have the mind of God. She gets her pleasure by doing her own thing. She loves and commits to her own self-will. Her commitment is to her own self. At the cost of others her main priority is to be number one. She is not spiritually aware of the consequences of being selfish and therefore, she greedily self indulges into her own wants and desires.

She often sees what she wants and rapidly goes after it. She doesn't care if someone else's home is broken and destroyed. She doesn't care about the well-being of the families she is destroying. She wants what she wants and very often she gets it.

The worldly woman has great ambitions and being labeled an opportunist fixes firmly to her personality without any ambiguity. But her ambitions are not from God. She doesn't care whom she may destroy. This woman's quality is of a great manipulator. She knows how to conquer and destroy her victim, without any remorse for the after effects. Having pleasure is just for fun. Her aim is not to please, but to be pleased by few or many. So when she is degraded by the opposite sex as being labeled 'a woman of the world' she does not relate. The woman of the world normally uses others as here label describes her.

Not yet being familiar with the god of this world, the worldly woman sometimes becomes the exact duplicate of her father the devil, and his motives are" to steal, to kill and to destroy." Paul writes in the Book of Romans 1: 18, 22-24, 26-27, which says, "For the wrath of God is revealed from heaven against all ungodliness and unrighteousness of men, who hold the truth in unrighteousness; Professing themselves to be wise, they became fools, and changed the glory of the uncorruptible God into an image made like to corruptible man, and to birds, and four-footed beasts, and creeping things. Wherefore God also gave them up to uncleanness through the lusts of their own hearts, to dishonor their own bodies between themselves. For this cause God gave them up unto vile affections for even their women did change the natural use into that which is against nature: And likewise also the men, leaving the natural lust of the woman, burned in their lust one toward another; men with men working that which is unseemly, and receiving in themselves that recompense of their error which was meet." Solomon speaks of this woman in Proverb 6:26 which says, "For by means of a whorish woman a man is brought to a piece of bread: and the adulteress will hunt for the precious life." The power of God breaks and destroys many yokes; this worldly woman has been many of the women that now call on the name of Jesus. I Corinthians 6:9-11 declares, "Know ye not that the unrighteous shall not inherit the kingdom of God? Be not deceived: neither fornicators, nor idolaters, nor adulterers, nor effeminate, nor abusers of themselves with mankind, nor thieves, nor covetous, nor drunkards, nor revilers, nor extortioners, shall inherit the kingdom of God. And such were some of you: but ye are washed, but ye are sanctified, but ye are justified in the name of the Lord Jesus, and in the Spirit of our God."

This woman of the world attracts people that are hungry for destruction. The worldly woman is experienced, sophisticated, and matured. This woman has worldly wisdom. James the brother of Jesus Christ, who is also considered the proverbial of the New Testament, declares that worldly wisdom is, "But if ye have bitter envying and strife (self-seeking), in your hearts, glory not, and lie not against the truth. This wisdom descendeth not from above, but is earthy, sensual, devilish. For where envying and strife (self-seeking) is, there is confusion and every evil work." (James 3:14-16). The worldly woman is knowledgeable.

She is well informed of what is going on in her world, and around her world. This woman is on the ball. She is informed about everybody else's business. By being disguised as a friend in deed, she knows how to creep into homes unawares. She even knows how to capture the captor. This worldly woman is a qualified veteran. She gets her instructions and directions from Satan, and she's an unexpected victim. She is capable of destroying, annihilating, and conquering men, women, and children. Everyone that comes into her presence she views them as a prey. She also has the outer appearance of glamour. But as Jesus quoted in Matthew 23:27,

> "Woe unto you, scribes, and Pharisees, hypocrites! For ye are like unto whited sepulchers, which indeed appear beautiful outward, but are within full of dead men's bones, and of all uncleanness."

The worldly woman has no shame in her game she is capable, competent, and clever. By being capable the worldly woman demonstrates that she is talented, intelligent and bright. By being competent she demonstrates that she is an expert in almost everything that she does. She also is proficiently skilled in manipulating others. Her cleverness makes her known as being quick and witty. The worldly woman does not let her guard down. She is focus, lively, and alert. She has the ability to manipulate anyone she has personal contact with. Because she tires easily of total commitment she only wants gratification for a season. This worldly woman knows how to use her knowledge of the world to persuade and conquer. She is flexible in her life desires and life styles. But thanks be to God that can save and will save the worldly woman and will make her a vessel of honor for His Glory.

Hallelujah God saved ME and You.

CHAPTER IV

The Holy
Woman

T here is a mandate from God to every Christian woman, which is quoted by many, but understood by few. The mandate is: "Sanctify yourselves therefore, and be ye holy: for I am the LORD your God. And ye shall keep my statutes, and do them: for I am the LORD which sanctify you." Leviticus 20:7

Holiness is a definite way of living. It is a lifestyle of shunning the wrong and doing what is right. The inner and outer garments do not sanctify a woman, but a holy woman sanctifies her garments. She dresses according to her love relationship with God. Her appeal is not to the god of this world, but her appeal is to draw others to the God of her life. This holy woman of God is worthy of high regards, because she greatly appreciates her salvation. This woman is admired, well regarded and blessed by God. To be called sanctified is not an embarrassment to her. She embraces and reserves sanctification. This woman of God has learned how to treasure the word sanctify.

She realizes that being known as 'set apart' is to highly esteem God. The holy woman knows how to endure. Life's experience has taught her that to waver and to be double minded will stunt her growth in God. Her life is empowered by the holiness of God. She has no room for compromise. The word compromise is an enemy to the woman of holiness. Her strength is in God, who constantly declares unto her, be ye holy, for I am holy. This holy woman of God will not tolerate sin in her life. She is constantly before God asking for forgiveness. She does not take any ill feelings for granted. The holy woman of God treasures and cherishes her salvation, that so often some Christians have said to her, "girl it doesn't take all that to be saved." What she lives in church she lives outside the walls of the Sanctuary. She positions herself on 1 John 1:9 which declares, "If we confess our sins, he is faithful, and just to forgive us our sins, and to cleanse us from all unrighteousness." She recognizes and appreciates the differences between right and wrong also evil and good. Therefore, with gratitude she values her relationship with God. She makes every effort not to have her good evil spoken of and not to bring any reproach to the Holy Name of God and the Body of Christ. This holy woman of God does not take bribes or gifts. She rehearses in her mind the scripture that states, "Gifts blind the eyes."

Her stance is "my God shall supply all my needs according to his riches in glory." The holy rhetoric that proceeds from her mouth, is "The LORD is my shepherd I shall not want." The Holy Ghost has formed words of trust within her heart for God, and therefore her commitment is to God. Without any hesitation or reservation she follows the instructions that says, "So leave the corruption and compromise, leave it for good," says God. "Don't link up with those who will pollute you. I want you all for myself." (II Corinthians 6:17 Complete Jewish Bible), and "I beseech you therefore, brethren, by the mercies of God, that ye present your bodies a living sacrifice, holy, acceptable unto God, which is your reasonable service." (Romans 12:1)

This holy woman of God has integrity and character. Therefore, she does not entertain single men without being appropriately, properly, decently, in the right way, and in good order chaperoned. She does not take money from men and others for the focus of possessions. She does not tantalize others to get what they got. She does not tease for the sake of unholy entertainment. Again this holy woman of God does not take bribes.

Her reverential fear of God will not allow her to commit fornication or adultery.

She is not perplexing. She does not have to prove to anyone that she is pure in her life style and conduct of holiness. Her strength and her purity come from God. This holy woman of God has learned how to commit her total being and her total desires to God who is the Author and Finisher of her faith. Henceforth, anyone or anything that does not possess God's character, she will not compromise her lifestyle of Godly living. Her fortitude is the word of God that declares, "I am persuaded that what I commit to him against that day he is able to keep it." This does not mean that desires are not there, sure they are. But the holy woman of God has decided to be an ensample to other women of God. She will wait for her Boaz. God says, "Wait on the LORD: be of good courage, and he shall strengthen thine heart: wait, I say on the LORD." (Psalm 27:14)

The Hebrew word 'wait' means qavah—which means to bind together, to expect, to look patiently, to tarry, and to wait. The word Courage in the Hebrew language means chazaq—to fasten upon to be strong, to cure, to help, to repair. I have used two words that will bring our waiting into perspective. Holy women of JEHOVAH do not give up; God is expecting us to attach ourselves with Him. We are to hope for and long for the promises of God. Our expectation of God should be everlasting to everlasting. Ephesians 3:20 says, "Now unto him that is able to do exceeding abundantly above all that we ask or think, according to the power that worketh in us."

Our courage is fastened upon God. We are to look to God for help. In order to be strong we need to ask God for His help. Most single women have been hurt in the past by innumerable bad experiences. To wait on God with great anticipation, we need to be healed, to be repaired, to be restored, and to be cured. We should allow Jehovah Rophe The Lord that heals us to come into our lives so that we might receive total restoration. Holy women of God need to be repaired, restored, and revived. There are seasons of healing for the holy woman. She should rest in the God of her salvation. Resting and Healing is a form of Salvation. As holy women of God we need to allow the Holy Ghost to give us a HOLY DOSE of forgiveness.

I am holy because God is HOLY.

CHAPTER V

The Purpose Of Being A Woman

*T*he word purpose means—to cause, incentive, motive, propose, and encouragement. "To everything there is a season, and a time to every purpose under the heaven" (Ecclesiastes 3:1). "Every purpose is established by counsel" (Proverb 21:18).

The Woman was made for a purpose. Adam was without a mate he had named every animal and every animal of its kind had its own mate. God saw that Adam was lonely and needed someone in his life. There is a need in the life of a man to be fulfilled. His very being of being empty and being unsound can only be fulfilled by 1) the fullness of God, and 2) The wholeness of a woman.

God made woman for a Divine purpose. We all know that God took Eve from one of the ribs of Adam, and Adam called her woman. The woman was not taken from many ribs if that was so, Adam would have had many wives at one time. We were created, formed to be by our husband's side. Woman was not created to be neither a door mate nor a slave. The woman's purpose was not intended to be physically abused, immorally abused, financially abused, emotionally abused, and verbally abused. Her purpose is to be loved by the God of her salvation.

Genesis 2:24 says, "Therefore shall a man leave his father and his mother, and shall cleave unto his wife: and they shall be one flesh. And they were both naked, the man and his wife, and were not ashamed." The very motive that God created woman, was that she should be loved and cherished by man. I am not just talking about any man, but the special man that God has already pre-ordained for this woman of God. In time past women have gotten into relationships that has question their reasoning of why are they here on planet earth. Often bad intense, inferior, regretful, immoral and rotten relationships can dampen, (suppress or suffocate) the very purpose, aim, design and intent of whom you are and why God allowed you to be born. God Almighty does not want us women to allow bad relationships and bad experiences to stop or hinder the very basis for our creation. We are created in the very likeness of God. "And God said, Let us make man in our image, after our likeness" (Genesis 1:26a).

There is no doubt or question about the motives of God. God's plans always come into fruition and completion. The design and plan that God devised for woman was and is to be the wife of one man, and to bear children. We are to be loved. We are not to be degraded or to be humiliated by words of insults and ignorance. We were created in the image and likeness of God. The word of God attributes these words to Adam, but we know that if he allowed Adam to go to sleep, and extracted from him a rib, and created for Adam his woman, then the same Word, which were committed (to make known the views of oneself), to Adam were also committed to Eve. "Male and female created he them; and blessed them, and called their name Adam, in the day were created." (Genesis 5:2).

The purpose of a woman that God created was already formatted in heaven.

God's design, plan or purpose for His woman is that she be "fearfully and wonderfully made."(Psalm 139.14). Any other type of union with a human being was not instituted nor purposed in the mind of God. Because the Word of God is eternally right and I will reiterate the Holiness of God in this book that a woman was made for a man. A woman was not made for others which are not a male; this is an abomination in the eyesight of God. Romans 1:24-26 says,

"Wherefore God also gave them up to uncleanness through the lusts of their own hearts, to dishonour their own bodies between themselves: Who changed the truth of God into a lie, and worshipped and served the creature more that the Creator, who is blessed forever. Amen. For this cause God gave them up unto vile affections for even their women did change the natural use into that which is against nature."

The purpose of God's woman is to reflect the magnificence of her creator. This woman of God was divinely designed to walk in the spirit of holiness every day that she abides here on earth. She is to reflect God's beauty and God's righteousness. Every since the beginning of time evil men came with vain imagination to have a woman make a living for him. This type of man does not work and will not work. A woman was not made to be immorally used by others. Every woman has chosen or may have been force into lifestyles that she did not permit or particular care for. Therefore, we realize that there have been some lifestyles that have not been promotional for the woman of God. The design and scheme of immortality brings in a stumbling block that may seem to hinder the very plan of God. A woman was created by God to be cherished, to be treated with affection and tenderness, to hold dear. For the reason we were created to be treasured, we will no longer compromise our existence of being holy and godly women. We will not permit others to be detrimental to our lifestyles of godly living. We are God's women.

We will present ourselves as 'worship' to God because we have received Jesus Christ in our lives as our personal Savior. No longer will we sabotage our bodies; no longer will we destroy our children. No longer will we allow anyone to take advantage of us, take advantage of our children and their children by their wicked lifestyles and actions.

Our purpose here is not to be another Delilah that scheme with the enemy, and who allowed the man of God to put his head in her lap to get what she needed to destroy the people of God.

Judges 16:6 says, "And Delilah said to Samson, Tell me I pray thee, wherein thy great strength lieth, and wherewith thou mightiest be out to afflict thee."

We will not be another Jezebel who scheme with her weak husband Ahab, to kill the man of God, just to get his vineyard. We are not witches and we will not practice witchcraft to get what we want or need.

1 King 21:7 says, "And Jezebel his wife said unto him, dost thou now govern the kingdom of Israel? Arise, and eat bread, and let thine heart be merry: I will give thee the vineyard of Naboth the Jezzreelite."

We will not be another Zeresh who scheme with her deceitful husband Haman to build the gallows, and desired that the king hanged Mordecai the man of God.

Esther 5:14 says, "Then said Zeresh his wife and all his friends unto him. Let a gallows be made of fifty cubits high, and tomorrow speak thou unto the king that Mordecai may be hanged thereon: then go thou in merrily with the king unto the banquet. And the thing pleased Haman: and he caused the gallows to be made."

We will not be another Job's wife, who told her husband to curse God and die.

Job 2:9 say, "Then said his wife unto him, Dost thou still retain thine integrity? Curse God and die." We will not be strange women. Proverb 5:3-4 says, "For the lips of a strange woman drop as a honeycomb, and her mouth is smoother than oil: But her end is bitter as wormwood, sharp as a two edged sword."

The Purpose of the holy woman is to serve the Lord with gladness. We desire to be women like Jabez's mother who bore her son in sorrow, yet he did not stay in sorrow, but demanded the blessings of God for his life. Jabez's mother gave birth to a son that grabbed hold on to God and God changed his world. 1 Chronicles 4:9-10 says, "And Jabez was more honorable than his brethren: and his mother called his name Jabez, saying, because I bare him with sorrow. And Jabez called on the God of Israel, saying, Oh that thou wouldest bless me indeed, and enlarge my coast, and that then hand might be with me, and that thou wouldest keep me from evil, that it may not grieve me! And God granted him that which he requested." Our purpose is to give life, and that life will change lives.

We desire to be women like Belshazzar's mother who was regarded as the noblest and most beautiful woman of her time. History records that Belshazzar's mother who was also known as the Queen Nitorcis did much to beautify Babylon. She built beautiful bridges, wharves, tiled embankments, and lakes. She also made improvements and enlargements to buildings. Years after her husband Nebuchadnezzar's death she was an influential force in the government. Daniel 5:10 says, "Now the queen by reason of the words of the king and his lords came into the banquet house: and the queen spake and said, O king live forever: let not thy thoughts trouble thee nor let thy countenance be changed."

As holy women of God our purpose is to be women who are beautiful and builders. We desire to be women like the four hundred young wives. These four hundred virgins were brought into the defeated Benjamites. This defeat came after the war, which started over the Ephraim Levite's concubine, who had been ill treated by the wicked sons of Benjamin who had no wives.

The Israelites found them wives amongst their own daughters. These good wives civilized the Benjamites influencing them to repair cities that they may dwell in them. Judges 21: 12a, 23 says,

> "And they found among the inhabitants of Jabesh-gilead four hundred young virgins, which had known no man by lying with any male. And the children of Benjamin did so, and took them wives, according to their number of them that danced, whom they caught: and they went and returned unto their inheritance, and repaired the cities, and dwelt in them."

Our purpose is being godly women that will influence good. We desire to be women like Jochebed the daughter of Levi, and the mother of Moses. This woman of God acknowledged that her faith trusted in the God of her people. She trusted God's providential care to provide care for her son floating down a marshy inlet.

"And there went a man of the house of Levi, and took to wife a daughter of Levi. And the woman conceived, and bare a son: and when she saw him that he was a goodly child, she hid him three months. Then said his sister to Pharaoh's daughter, shall I go and call to thee a nurse of the Hebrew women that she may nurse the child for thee? And Pharaoh's daughter said to her, go. And the maid went and called the child's mother" (Exodus 2:1, 7-8).

Our purpose is to not to accent the situation, but to accentuate our faith and trust God.

Women, God has declared in his Holy Word that we were made for His divine purpose.

The Word of God gives many scripture illustration of women of purpose. The scriptures have inherent testimonies of women that lived the plans of God. God has presented to each woman a proposal.

This proposal is to be all that God has us to be. He wants us to tap into his Divine plan, and Divine design.

The woman of purpose must be submissive to the things of God. She cannot give up hope. She must know that God has a structure for her life. It is up to each woman to walk into the structured plans of God. Realizing that God is all knowing, we as women must understand the purpose of God.

And that purpose is encouraging.

We are encouraged because we know that the future holds incentives for our lives. Our incentives are that we are pressing towards an enhanced life. Our life will not only be worthwhile and wholesome in heaven, but it will be meaningful and skillful here on earth. Therefore, we look for the purposes and the plans of God. We search diligently for God's ideas, thoughts, and methods. Jeremiah 29:11, has much value

Which says, "For I know the thoughts that I think toward you, saith the LORD, thoughts of peace, and not of evil, to give you an expected end." Women of purpose everything God has for us has already been mapped out, no longer will we struggle with our identity. We know who we are; we are the sons of God. Ephesians 4:1-3 says,

"I therefore, the prisoner of the Lord, beseech you that ye walk worthy of the vocation wherewith ye are called. With all lowliness and meekness, with longsuffering, forbearing one another in love; Endeavoring to keep the unity of the Spirit in the bond of peace."

Chapter VI

*F*ree

The definition for free or freedom is almost the same but not quite synonymous. To be free means—gratis, free of charge, for nothing, on the house, without payment, without charge, complimentary, flattering, admiring, kind, gracious, and approving. Whereas freedom means liberty, free will, choice, self-determination, autonomy—which means sovereignty, self-government, self-sufficiency, self rule, independence.

Every woman wants and desires to be free. They will do anything to obtain and receive their freedom. To be free and to have the freedom for women have been a right that has been a controversy since the beginning of time. Eve wanted her freedom when she did not obey God. She desired certain rights. And she desired to be free by listening and obeying a creature that was completely against God.

We have studied 19th century women, which triumphed over state and federal laws that discriminated against women rights.

These laws posed some of the most significant obstacles to securing women's rights. The earliest campaign to receive and to improve women's legal status in the United States centered on gaining property rights for women. Property rights for women have always been an issue

Genesis 3:1-6 says,

"Now the serpent was more subtile than any beast of the field which the LORD God had made. And he said unto the woman, Yea, hath God said, Ye shall not eat of every tree of the garden? And the woman said unto the serpent, We may eat of the fruit of the trees of the garden: But of the fruit of the tree which is in the midst of the garden, God hath said, Ye shall not eat of it, neither shall ye touch it, let ye die. And the serpent said unto the woman, Ye shall not surely die. For God doth know that in the day ye eat thereof, then your eyes shall be opened, and ye shall be as gods, knowing good and evil. And when the woman saw that the tree was good for food, and that it was pleasant to the eyes, and a tree to be desired to make one wise, she took of the fruit thereof, and did eat, and gave also unto her husband with her; and he did eat."

Eve wanted property rights but she set out to obtain it in the wrong way. We have had American women's rights activists such as Elizabeth Cady Stanton, and Susan B. Anthony, which fought for the right to vote. They argued that 14th Amendment conferred on women constitutional equality and the rights of full citizenship. Great women such as Senator Margaret Chase Smith and Congresswoman Martha Griffiths led the campaign to free women in the labor legislation. All these women played an important role to free women and to have the freedom of womanhood.

Let's consider the freedom fighter Harriett Tubman known as 'Moses of the Civil War'. Her life was to be free from slavery, and to enjoy the freedom God had given her. A portion of the article that was written about her states, "a mystic railroad without tracks wound its way across America over one hundred and fifty years ago. The railroad, nicknamed the Underground Railroad, was a misnomer because it was neither underground nor a railroad. The slaves were aided by thousands of "conductors" who used covered wagons or carts with false bottoms to carry slaves from one station to another. There were many famous conductors such as: Salmon P. Chase, who as Chief

Justice of the Supreme Court would later preside over Andrew Johnson's impeachment; Elijah F Pennypacker; Lucretia Mott; Levi Coffin; the charismatic Frederick Douglass; and the legendary Harriet Tubman. Harriett Tubman earned the name Moses for her heroic exploits in leading slaves to the Promised Land. Harriett Tubman continued her courageous exploits during the Civil War. Millions of slaves admired her brave life and many escaped slaves who owed their freedom to Tubman probably felt as Harriett Tubman did when she said, "I looked at my hands to see if I was the same person now that I was free."

This was a woman that brought a tremendous amount of people from slavery to freedom.

The Holy Bible tells us about a man named Moses. God commissioned this man to go back down into Egypt and inform Pharaoh to let his people go. God honored his word. He brought the children out of bondage to serve and to worship him. There is a natural freedom, and there is a spiritual freedom. To be free in the natural helps every woman to accomplish material possessions. To be free in the spiritual gives every woman the confidence of being a conqueror. We need both freedoms to be all that God has predestined for us. John 8:31-32 says,

> "Then said Jesus to those Jews which believed on him, If ye continue in my word, then are ye my disciples indeed: And ye shall know the truth, and the truth shall make you free."

We have been bought with a price. Every Christian woman has been ransomed from the very dredge hole of hell initiated by Satan. We are free to proclaim Jesus' name. We are no longer under bondage to the slave masters of the two worlds. We are slaves to our Lord and Savior Jesus Christ. We are free to serve Him in the beauty of holiness. We are free to praise and worship his name. We are free to live a life of integrity and character. We are free to dance before his graciousness without shame. We are free to be flattering, admiring, approving, and encouraging. Therefore, because of our freedom we are self-sufficient, self-govern, and self-rule in Christ Jesus. Women that are free symbolize independence. Our being independent does not exempt us from being totally dependent on God. Women that are free constantly trust in, rely on, hope for, and have faith in God. Jesus who is our Moses, our deliverer has freed us from the destruction and the misery of hell.

Women that are free will not be bound by circumstances, disappointments, distresses, misfortunes, mishaps, heartaches or heartbreaks. As women of the Most Highest God, we appreciate the women rights' activists, and the women rights' movements. We appreciate the many women who fought for and cross over race and political barricades for what they believe in regarding women's' rights. These barriers and stumbling blocks were challenges that were overcome by women that leaped and stepped into their freedom.

WOMEN FREEDOM AND LIBERATION

PROPERTY RIGHTS—NY STATE PASSED THE MARRIED PROPERTY ACT IN 1848

UNDER THE INFLUENCE OF THE NATIONAL WOMEN'S PARTY, THE US CONGRESS INTRODUCED THE ERA IN 1923

THE COMMISSION ON THE STATUS OF WOMEN LED DIRECTLY TO THE PASSAGE OF THE EQUAL PAY ACT IN 1963

UNDER THE INSPIRITAION OF THE HOLY GHOST, JOEL 2:28-29 SAYS,

"AND IT SHALL COME TO PASS AFTERWARD, THAT I WIIL POUR OUT MY SPIRIT UPON ALL FLESH, AND YOUR SONS AND YOUR DAUGHTERS SHALL PROPHESY, YOUR OLD MEN SHALL DREAM DREAMS, YOUR YOUNG MEN SHALL SEE VISIONS. AND ALSO UPON THE SERVANTS AND UPON THE HANDMAIDS (WOMEN) IN THOSE DAYS WILL I POUR OUT MY SPIRIT." DATE FROM EVERLASTING TO EVERLATING

CHAPTER VII

Faithful Woman

*B*eing faithful is a reactionary response of obedience out of love, towards someone that has demonstrated inner qualities of exactness, soundness, truthfulness, and wholesomeness.

A woman will not be faithful to another unless that person has already exemplified characteristic of being honest and upright. A woman is faithful because she loves the man of her life, not because of her obligation to him. She doesn't wants to be obligated in her love. In order to be faithful there has to be a symbol of strength and stability. The person that is receiving the gift of loyalty must be anchored in their character and fortitude.

The Encarta Dictionary definition of the faithful means—true, realistic, genuinely real, credible, reliable, constant, dependable, loyal and predictable.

There was a time in the history of our nation that immigrants came to America.

The definition for immigrant means—someone who has come to another country and settled there.

The greatest influx of immigrants to the United States occurred between the 1840s and the 1920s.

During this era, approximately 37 million immigrants arrived in the United States. The reason of the 19th century immigration was Industrialization in Europe, which caused relocation.

The transformation from small, agriculture-based societies to manufacturing economies was so rapid and sweeping that it became known as the Industrial Revolution. Economic changes were the predominant factors prompting these movements; others also left their homelands because of political upheavals, religious persecution, or in search of adventure. The diversity of nationality, which came from countries such as: England, Scotland, Wales, Germany, Italy, and Israel came seeking for extraordinary greatness.

They left their misery, their impoverishment, and their being forsaken behind them. They wanted incredible more than what they had already lived.

So women who are faithful have the same ideas, motivations, and thoughts because,

"Ye are of God, little children, and have overcome the world: because greater in he that is in you than he that is in the world" (I John 4:4)

Their arrival to the land of the free was not disappointing to them. They had become free and now were arriving to their destiny, which was 'freedom'.

High and lifted up the Statue was erected to welcome them. This Statue was called Liberty.

The Statue of Liberty stands as a welcoming symbol to millions of immigrants to the United States for more than 100 years.

At 151 feet in height she is one of the largest statues in the world. She is probably also the most recognized statue in the world.

Lady Liberty was conceived way back in 1865 by a group of French scholars and statesman who were enjoying a dinner meal together in Glatigny, France. These men were ardent admirers of the American system, especially its Constitution. It was suggested that a gift be sent to the American people, by way of giving homage to that nation as well as marking its centennial celebration.

The woman with the flowing robe holding a flaming torch in her raised hand is still there. As of today, she hasn't gone anywhere. Her strength and nobility is still infamous amongst many immigrants. With her faithful stand she has encouraged and welcomes many. The famous Statue of Liberty is still standing. As women of God we should have the same endurance and that is to be faithful (standing).

Like the Statue of Liberty, we as Christian women will weather the storms of this world. We will experience the seasons of Winter, Spring, Summer, and Fall. No matter what season we are in we will strengthen ourselves with the promises of God. Being faithful is a character and attribute of God.

> Because God is faithful we must be faithful to him. The Word of God says, "It is of the LORD'S mercies that we are not consumed, because his compassions fail not. They are new every morning; great is thy faithfulness." (Lamentation 3:22-23)

God is faithful to us, therefore, as Christian women we must be faithful to God. Although we are in many waters, yet the waters will not overtake us.

The excited Frenchman Bartholdi built the Statue of Liberty. His creation soon came to incorporate the symbols of its maker's personal life views. Lady Liberty took on symbols including a book, the torch in her left hand, and the seven pointed diadem around her head.

How much more Christian women should take on the personal and spiritual life views of our Creator God Almighty. The symbol of the book is the Word of God—Jesus Christ who is the Author And Finisher of our faith. The symbol of the torch is the fire of God—The Holy Ghost. The symbol of the seven-pointed diadem is the Glory of God.

The symbol of being faithful is what God Almighty is all about. He declared in his word,

> "Let your conversation be without covetousness; and be content with such things as ye have: for he hath said, I will never leave thee, nor forsake thee. So that we may boldly say, THE LORD IS MY HELPER, AND I WILL NOT FEAR WHAT MAN SHALL DO UNTO ME" (Hebrews 13:5-6).

In Kay Arthur's book 'From God's Heart To Yours, she penned Nothing Too Difficult. This is regarding her desire to have a husband. Here is an insert of what she wrote. I titled by paper. "On Hunting Husbands and Winning Wives," and in it I showed, first of all how God sends His Holy Spirit out to obtain a bride for His Son, the Lord Jesus Christ. Then I explained how God, because He is omnipresent, could search the whole world over and find the perfect mate for each of us. Christian women we should be faithful to God in our walk, and in our talk. There should be no place for compromising our Christian standards. Glorifying God in our bodies is a prerequisite for receiving the promises made by Him.

We are faithful to serve Him, we are faithful to live holy before Him, and we are faithful to worship Him. There is no room in our lives for immorality involvement before marriage. What God has promised is exactly what he will perform.

"God is not a man that he should lie; neither the son of man that he should repent: hath he said, and shall he not do it? Or hath he spoken, and shall he not make it good?" (Numbers 22:19). Again we may have desires and wants for Winter season, but God has already plan to give us the same desires and wants during the Spring Summer, and Fall seasons.

"For I know the thoughts that I think toward you, saith the LORD, thoughts of peace, and not of evil, to give you an expected end. Then shall ye call upon me, and ye shall go and pray unto me, and I will hearken unto you. And ye shall seek me, and find me, when ye shall search for me with all your heart.

And I will be found of you saith the LORD: and I will turn away your captivity, and I will gather you from all the nations and from all the places whither I have driven you, saith the LORD, and I will bring you again into the place whence I caused you to be carried away" (Jeremiah 29:11-14).

Even as the Statue of Liberty stands without bending or folding, we also as Christian women must stand without bending or folding. To the many immigrants that came from far off lands, looking for a symbol of hope. We too have come from far off lands looking for hope.

We have found hope in the faithful God. "Jesus Christ in you the hope of glory."

"Wherefore, remember, that ye being in time past Gentiles in the flesh, who are called Uncircumcision by that which is called the Circumcision in the flesh made by hands; That at that time ye were without Christ, being aliens (immigrants) from the commonwealth of Israel, and strangers from the covenants of promise, having no hope (no country), and without God in the world: But now in Christ Jesus ye who sometimes were far off are made nigh by the blood of Christ" (Ephesians 2:11-13).

The Statue of Liberty is, indeed, a much-cherished gift. If only the ideals that she stands for, life, liberty and peace, were a reality in her homeland, then her existence would have real meaning.

As Christian women we will imitate (follow) the God of our salvation. Paul writes to the Ephesians be ye therefore followers imitators of God in forgiving and loving. O how much more to be an imitator of God, than of Homer, Virgil or Alexander The Great.

5:3   But let not any impure love be even named or heard of among you—Keep at the utmost distance from it, as becometh saints.

5:4   Nor foolish talking—Tittle tattle, talking of nothing, the weather, fashions, meat and drink. Or jesting—The word properly means, wittiness, facetiousness, esteemed by the heathens an half—virtue. But how frequently even this quenches the Spirit, those who are tender of conscience know. Which are not convenient—For a Christian; as neither increasing his faith nor holiness.

5:6   Because of these things—As innocent as the heathens esteem them, and as those dealers in vain words would persuade you to think them.

5:8   Ye were once darkness—Total blindness and ignorance. Walk as children of light—Suitably to your present knowledge.

There are examples of faithful monuments and people in our history such as:

1. Mount Rushmore—which has been called the "The Shrine of Democracy." The granite faces of four American presidents' tower 5,500 feet above sea level and is scaled to men who would stand who stand 465 feet tall. President Calvin Coolidge believes Mount Rushmore was "decidedly American in its conception, magnitude and meaning.

2. Empire State Building—New York City, skyscraper located on 5th Avenue between 33rd and 34 streets, which when it was completed in 1931, was the tallest building in the world. At 1250ft it no longer holds that distinction, having been surpassed in height by several structures both in the United States and in Asia. Because of its elegant stepped design it is often still regarded as the ultimate American skyscraper.

3. The Grand Canyon—No matter how much people have heard about the Grand Canyon, seeing the real thing makes them gasp. They gaze in awe at its huge vista and stunning depth, with every color of the rainbow in the rocks. "Grand seems almost too small a term for this utterly spectacular place. One of the largest gorges on Earth, it is a 277-mile red slash through the green and yellow of the surrounding plateau.

4. The Golden Gate Bridge—is the entrance to the San Francisco bay from the Pacific Ocean. The strait is approximately three-miles long by one-mile wide with currents ranging from 4.5 to 7.5 knots. It is generally accepted that the strait was named "Chrysopulae", or Golden Gate, by John C. Fremont, Captain, and topographical Engineers of the U.S. Army circa 1846. It reminded him of a harbor in Istanbul named Chrysoceras or Golden Horn

5. Black Women Of The Old West—
    a. Sojourner Truth—a voiced raised against human bondage and for women's rights.
    b. Sara Jane Woodson—the first black graduate of Oberlin College in Ohio to become a teacher.

c. African American women owned Beverly Hills California, and others owned huge parcels of Los Angeles real estate.

d. Luticia Parson—a nurse for the Buffalo Soldiers in the Southwest.

e. Aviatrix Bessie Coleman, born in Texas, was unable to find a flying instructor in the United States. She gained her French pilot's license in 1921 when she was only 25.

Those who gave their lives and built great landmarks were faithful to their assignments. But we have a greater assignment, which has been given to us by God. Being faithful to God is not being rational, nor is it being an empiricist.

As, faithful women we do not have to rationalize God commandments in our minds. Therefore, we do not have to feel, see, taste, or touch to be faithful

We believe the Word of God, and believing just what God has said through the living and written word, which is The Logos of God. Hebrews 12:1 says,

"Wherefore seeing we also are compassed about with so great a cloud of witnesses, let us lay aside every weight, and the sin which doth so easily beset us, and let us run with patience the race that is set before us.

We are faithful to God, because by faith the elders obtained a good report. By faith Abel offered unto God a more excellent sacrifice than Cain. By faith Enoch was translated that he should not see death. By faith Noah, being warned of God of things not seen as yet, moved with fear, prepared an ark to the saving of his house" (Hebrews 11:1a, 2a, 5a, 7a).

We know that there is life, liberty and peace in The Faithful God. The feminine free woman has been commissioned to be faithful and to live a holy life in the presence of God.

Summary

WOMEN OF THE HIGHEST GOD THERE IS A STANDARD THAT WE MUST EXEMPLIFY TO THE WORLD. GODLY WOMEN ARE SO PRECIOUS IN GOD'S SIGHT. THEREFORE, WE MUST LIVE UP TO THE EXPECTATION THAT GOD HAS POSITIONED UPON US.

GOD'S WOMAN LIVES A LIFE THAT WILL BRING GREAT HONOR TO HER KING. SO MANY WOMEN HAVE FAILED GOD, BECAUSE THEY HAVE THOUGHT IN THEIR FINITE MIND THAT LIVING A HOLY AND GODLY LIFE IS IMPOSSIBLE. THERE IS NOTHING IMPOSSIBLE WITH GOD. SOMEONE IS BANKING ON YOU. THERE IS A LOST SOUL WHICH COULD BE EITHER A MAN OR WOMAN, WHO IS LOOKING FOR SOMEONE TO LIVE WHAT THEY TEACH OR PREACH.

ROMANS 12:1 SAYS,

'I BESEECH YOU THEREFORE, BRETHREN, BY THE MERCIES OF GOD, THAT YE PRESENT YOUR BODIES A LIVING SACRIFICE, HOLY, ACCEPTABLE UNTO GOD, WHICH IS YOUR REASONABLE SERVICE."

LIVE THE LIFE!!!!!!!!!!

Bibliography

1. ARTHUR, KAY. BELOVED FROM GOD'S HEART TO YOURS. EUGENE OREGON: HARVEST HOUSE PIBLISHERS, 1994
2. BARTER JAMES. THE Golden Gate BRIDGE. SAN DIEGO, CALIF: LUCENT BOOKS, 2001
3. BENTLEY, JUDITH. HARIET TUBMAN. NEW YORK: FRANKLIN WATTS INC, 1990
4. BLASHFIELD, JEAN F. AMERICA THE BEAUTIFUL/ ARIZONA. ARIZONA: CHILDREN'S PRESS, 2000
5. BRADFORD, SARAH. HARRIET TUBMAN THE MOSES OF HER PEOPLE. BEDFORD MASS: APPLEWOOD BOOKS, 1886
6. BRIMMER, LARRY DAVE. ANGEL ISLAND, NEW YORK: CHILDREN'S PRESS, 2001
7. CHEEK, LARRY. ARIZONA. OAKLAND, CALIF: COMPASS AMERICAN GUIDES INC, 1991
8. COLLINS, GARY R. CHRISTIAN COUNSELING. DALLAS: WORD PUBLISHING, 1988
9. DEEN, EDITH. ALL OF THE WOMEN OF THE BIBLE. NEW YORK: HARPER & ROW PUBLISHERS, 1955
10. DUMBECK, KRISTINA. LEADERS OF WOMEN SUFFRAGE. SAN DIEGO, CALIF: LUCENT BOOKS INC, 2001

11. FONE, BYRNE. HOMOPHOBIA, NEW YORK: METROPOLITAN BOOKS, 2000

12. HANKE, HOWARD A. THE THOMPSON CHAIN-REFERENCE BIBLE SURVEY. WACO, TEXAS: WORD BOOKS, 1981

13. INTERNET RESOURCES: JOHN DARBY'S SYNOPSIS OF THE BIBLE; WESLEY'S EXPLANATORY NOTES; GILLS EXPOSITION OF THE BIBLE

14. KATZ, WILLLIAM LOREN. BLACK WOMEN OF THE OLD WEST. NEW YORK: ANTHENEUM BOOKS FOR YOUNG READERS, 1995

15. KENDALL, MARTHA E. FAILURE IS IMPOSSIBLE. MINNEAPOLIS: LERNER PUBLICATION, 2001

16. LANGER, FREDDIE. THE EMPIRE STATE BUILDING. PRESTEL PUBLISHING, 2001

17. LOOS, PAMELA. ELIZABETH CADY STANTIN. BROOMHILL, PA: CHELSEA HOUSE PUBLISHING, 2000

18. MICHAELS, LISA. GRAND AMBITION. NEW YORK: W.W. NORTON, 2001

19. NELSON, THOMAS. THE KING JAMES STUDY BIBLE. NASHVILLE: THOMAS NELSON INC PUBLISHERS, 1975

20. NEUMANN, DIETRICH. JOE AND THE SKYCRAPER: THE EMPIRE STATE BUILDING IN NEW YORK CITY. MUNICH; NEW YORK: PRESTEL, 1999

21. PETERSEN, DAVID. GRAND CANYON NATIONAL PARK. NEW YORK: CHILDREN'S PRESS, 2001

22. SAGAN, MIRIAM, WORLD HISTORY SERIES/ WOMEN'S SUFFRAGE. SAN DIEGO, CALIF: LUCENT BOOKS, 1954

23. SANTELLA, ANDREW. CORNERSTONE OF FREEDOM/MOUNT RUSHMORE. NEW YORK: CHILDREN'S PRESS, 1999

24. SHERR, LYNN. FAILURE IMPOSSIBLE. NEW YORK: TIMES BOOKS, 1995

25. SEIDMAN, DAVID. CIVIL RIGHTS. NEW YORK: ROSEN PUB GROUP, 2001
26. TARUNAC, JOHN. THE MAKING OF A LANDMARK. ST MARTINS PRESS INC, 1997
27. THOMPSON, FRANK CHARLES. THE THOMPSON CHAIN REFERENCE BIBLE. INDIANAPOLIS, INDIANA: B.B. KIRKBRIDE BIBLE CO, 1982
28. WILLIAMS, MARY E. ABORTION. SAN DIEGO, CALIF: GREENHAVEN PRESS, 2002
29. WILLAMS, MARY E. HOMOSEXUALITY. SAN DIEGO, CALIF: GREENHAVEN PRESS, 1999
30. WEISBERG, BARBARA. SUSAN B ANTHONY. NEW YORK; PHILADELPHIA: CHELSEA HOUSE, 1988

Printed in the United States
By Bookmasters